Railways &
Recollections 1955

Contents

© John Stretton and Peter Townsend 2010

British Library Cataloguing in Publication Data
A catalogue record for this book is available from the British Library. Printed and bound in Great Britain

First published in 2010
ISBN 978 1 85794 337 5

Silver Link Publishing Ltd
The Trundle
Ringstead Road
Great Addington
Kettering
Northants NN14 4BW

Tel/Fax: 01536 330588
email: sales@nostalgiacollection.com
Website: www.nostalgiacollection.com

Frontispiece: **TYSELEY** 6 August 1955 and the summer Saturday specials are in full flow, attracting the attention of two young trainspotters on this platform. Bearing the code to alert signalmen of precisely which train this is, No 6302 has the appropriate express passenger lamp code as it glides gracefully into the station complex. No doubt pressed into service to help cope with the extra holiday traffic, it is here allocated to Reading shed. Apart from a month at Banbury in the spring of 1953, Reading was to be its home for many years until it moved away, for a final 2½ year stint at Didcot and withdrawal on 24 March 1962. *Gerald Adams, MJS collection*

Acknowledgements

First and foremost we would like to record our gratitude to the late Ray Ruffell without whom this book would not have been possible.

Your authors are indebted to their good friend Tom Ferris for invaluable assistance with the *Irish Interlude* section of this volume. Tom has written several books on Irish railways and his willingness to share his knowledge and enthusiasm is very much appreciated.

So many other people have helped - with snippets and guidance, facts and information - space, and space alone, precludes mention of them all, so THANK YOU ALL!

Opposite background: **KEGWORTH** As well as enjoying special trips over the UK's rail network, enthusiasts have also been keen to sample the rather different spectacle and experience of steam hauled special runs on industrial sites. One such was British Gypsum's network at Kingston-on-Soar and the run from there to Kegworth in Leicestershire, on the Midland Main Line. During the visit organised by the RCTS on 24 September, 1926-vintage Peckett 0-4-0ST *Lady Angela* provides interest and photographic opportunities. After being replaced by diesels, she was bought by the Midland Railway Society and moved to Shackerstone in 1971 for preservation. *Gerald Adams, MJS collection*

Introduction

1955 was a momentous year in the annals of the UK's railways, although not immediately obvious on the ground. For this was the year of the now infamous 'Modernisation Plan' from British Railways - eagerly awaited and feared in equal measure at the time. However, in the short term, things continued in their sweet way in day to day operations. Just seven years in from Nationalisation and the creation of `British Railways` (BR), there were still great numbers of ancient steam locomotives in everyday use, alongside 'Standard' types, many of which were still being built.

This latest volume in the ongoing ~'Railways & Recollections' series portrays the state of our railways in that fateful year, incorporating scenes throughout the UK, including Isle of Man and Ireland. As will be seen, the railway world, a mere decade after the end of WWII, was a very different place to what we see today.

In 1955, the country was beginning to see real green shoots of recovery from the post-War devastation and a move out of the dark days of deficiencies that had been endured so far. Rationing for food and clothing had ended (from 4 July 1954); shops were stocking new inventions and labour saving devices, some of which had been forshadowed in the 1951 'Festival of Britain'; seeds of a musical revolution were sown, that would literally rock and finally destory the status quo in popular culture; theatre and publishing were progressing, with new authors coming to the fore; and for one of your authors, it was also a momentous year - as he began trainspotting and a love affair with railways that has lasted to this day, as strong as ever! Your other author spent much of Christmas 1955 wandering the house, claiming that Father Christmas had taken the *Triang* train set down the wrong chimney! It went next door, but patience was rewarded the following Christmas, with a *Hornby* three rail set!

Elsewhere, it was a year of rail strikes over pay and conditions that led to the Government declaring a state of emergency; a tragic crash and death toll in the the LeMans 24-hour road race; Ruth Ellis became the last woman to be hanged in the UK for murder; the Festiniog Railway officially opened, as the UK's first preserved railway; 'Lolita' was published; and newsreaders first appeared on UK TV. Among 'personalities', Rowan Atkinson and Kevin Costner were born and James Dean was killed in a car crash.

We trust you will enjoy this glimpse at 1955 and that it will bring back many memories for those 'young' enough to have been there and that it will provide a fascinating insight for those too young to have those first hand recollections. The series is growing and we look forward to bringing you, our valued readers, more years to enjoy over the months ahead.

Peter Townsend
Northamptonshire

John Stretton
Gloucestershire

April 2010

Below: **BELFAST** By 1955, all that survived of the 80 - odd route miles of the former Belfast & Northern Counties Railway was the 12 mile long branch to the seaside resort and commuter town of Bangor. The rest of the system was closed within two years of it being acquired by the government of Northern Ireland's Ulster Transport Authority in 1948. While the Bangor line achieved the distinction in 1953 of being the first in the British Isles to be entirely operated by diesel traction, redundant former B&CDR steam locomotives lingered for a while around the former steam shed at Queen's Quay station in Belfast. 4-4-2 tank No 217 (the UTA added 200 to the original B&CDR numbers) which was built by Beyer Peacock in Manchester in 1909, last ran in 1953 and was scrapped in 1956, is believed to be the only B&CDR loco to have received the UTA's lined black livery and crest, the latter is on the cab.

Opposite page: **BELFAST** From the cab of one of the MED units arriving at Queen's Quay on a service from Bangor, another of the units is seen awaiting its next turn of duty. Queen's Quay, which opened originally in 1848 and was completely rebuilt between 1910 and 1913, was a substantial terminus with an overall roof and five platforms. With the closure of the lines to Newcastle and Donaghadee in 1950, it was certainly underused by this time and some of the arms on the impressive gantry, or the bridge of signals as the BCDR referred to it, have already been removed. The bridge of signals and 100 lever Belfast Yard Signal Cabin, seen on the right of the picture, both dated from the early twentieth century rebuilding of the station. The box controlled the line as far as Ballymacarrett Junction where the main line to Newcastle diverged and the connection from the Great Northern Railway system, via the erstwhile Belfast Central line, trailed in. This link was closed in 1965 but reopened in 1976 when the line was rebuilt and trains from both Bangor and the former GNR main line ran through to the new Belfast Central station, built on the site of the GNR's goods and cattle yard at Maysfield, beside the River Lagan. Both Queen's Quay and the GNR station at Great Victoria Street were closed at this time.

An Irish Interlude

Opposite: **BELFAST** Queen's Quay station. The UTA had taken a cautious decision to convert Bangor line services to Diesel Multiple Unit (DMU) operation and firstly borrowed units from the Great Northern Railway (Ireland). Following this favourable first step, the next step was to take three loco hauled carriages into their works at Duncrue Street and convert them into a prototype 3-car DMU. Each power car being fitted with two AEC underfloor engines; AEC also provided engines for railcars and driving units on the Great Western Railway. The prototype entered service on the route early in 1952 and a further fourteen sets, this time with Leyland-Walker engines, were built over the next two years and by 1954 virtually all Bangor line services were DMU hauled.

Already by 1955, Queen's Quay was a sad shadow of its former self. The overall roof has been removed and the canopy which would later provide some shelter for passengers on the island platform, has not yet been erected. Two of the MED units are seen on 23 August 1955. These were built by the UTA in Belfast using the frames of former LMS coaches, the design being based on two prototypes acquired from AEC in 1951. The MEDs could run in three or six car formations and had sliding recessed doors controlled by the guard, similar to those used on London Transport tube trains at the time. For those too young to remember Virol was still widely advertised at the time. One such advertisement in the late 1800s included a clue to its ingredients:

> 'A Preparation of BONE-MARROW
> An ideal form of fat for children and invalids'

a quote credited, in the advert, to *The Lancet.*

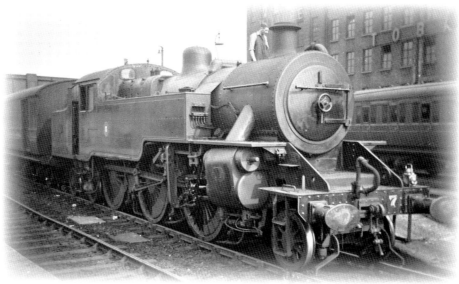

Above: **BELFAST** The Great Northern Railway's Belfast terminus at Great Victoria Street played host to an unusual visitor on 23rd August 1955 in the form of ex LMS/NCC WT class 2-6-4 tank, No 7. This was one of a class of eighteen locomotives constructed at Derby works. The first batch of ten, including No 7, were built for its Ulster offshoot by the LMS in 1946 and 1947, the remaining eight were built after nationalisation under the auspices of British Railways at Derby in 1949/50. Three survivors of this class which were affectionately known to both railwaymen and enthusiasts as the Jeeps because of their power and versatility, were among the last steam locomotives to remain in railway company service in these islands. Nos 4, 51 and 53 were not withdrawn by Northern Ireland Railways, the successor to the UTA, until 1971, three years after the end of steam on British Railways. No 4 was subsequently preserved by the Railway Preservation Society of Ireland and has travelled all over the island hauling RPSI railtours.

Top right: **BELFAST** On 23 August, the GNR's only diesel locomotive is seen at the company's Great Victoria Street terminus. This 0-8-0 diesel hydraulic built by Maschinenbau Kiel (MAK) in 1954 was initially supplied on trial to the GNR Board, at the maker's expense. It had an 800hp MAK diesel engine, Voith hydraulic transmission and weighed 57 tons. The locomotive had a theoretical top speed of 50 mph but with its eight coupled wheels, it had more the look of a shunter than a main line locomotive. It ran at first unnumbered but when the GNRB agreed to buy it, the locomotive was given the number 800. When the GNRB was abolished in 1958, its assets being divided between CIE and the UTA, the MAK went to CIE who renumbered it K801. Withdrawn from service in 1976, it was sold to a scrap metal company at Oranmore near Galway who used the engine to power car crushing machinery. The remains of this unique locomotive lingered on at the scrapyard until the late 1990s.

Right: **BELFAST** Abandoned UTA 4-6-4T No 223 stands forlornly outside Queen's Quay shed. Officially withdrawn the following year, this was one of the quartet of handsome and well proportioned 4-6-4 or Baltic tanks delivered by Beyer, Peacock & Co to the Belfast & County Down Railway in 1920. Incidentally, this Manchester firm was only surpassed in the number of steam locomotives it supplied to Ireland's railways by Inchicore works in Dublin. The BCDR Baltics flattered to deceive, having the reputation of possessing a prodigious appetite for coal whilst failing to deliver the power which might reasonably have been expected in return. Originally allocated the number 23 by the BCDR, it was renumbered 223 in 1951 by the Ulster Transport Authority. The 4-6-4 wheel arrangement was not common on the railways of the British Isles, the only other example in Ireland was supplied to the narrow gauge County Donegal Railway.

BELFAST The unique feature of the 'Enterprise Express', which first ran in August 1947, was that it could travel non-stop between Belfast and Dublin, because customs examinations were made at either terminus and not by stopping the train at the border. It proved so popular that a second service was soon introduced and between 1950 and 1953,

'The Enterprise' was extended to Cork. Both steam and diesel traction was used on the 'Enterprise'. Here, a set of GNR AEC railcars led by No 619 will shortly form a departure for Dublin. These railcars supplied in 1948 were at the time the most sophisticated diesel trains in these islands. Today the name Enterprise not only survives but is used as a brand which is

applied to the whole Belfast to Dublin service. Whilst there are more trains today, because they now serve several intermediate stations and no longer run non-stop, the timings are not much quicker than the best offered in the GNR era.

BELFAST A three car MED set leaves Queen's Quay for Bangor. Elsewhere in the British Isles such units would be referred to as DMUs (diesel multiple units) but in Ireland the tradition has always been to refer to these types of vehicles as railcars. The Irish railway operators were ahead of their colleagues across the Irish Sea when it came to the introduction of diesel traction. Yet even though the Great Northern were running express diesel railcar services from 1948, the Bangor line had been completely dieselised by 1953 and steam had effectively been abandoned in the Irish Republic by 1963, a few steam locomotives remained in service

in Northern Ireland until 1970/71. Most of the BCDR steam locomotives were tank engines of various vintages which were suitable for this compact system whose mainly passenger trains covered relatively short distances. Only one BCDR locomotive has survived, 4-4-2

tank No 30, built by Beyer Peacock in 1901, which is now preserved at the Ulster Folk & Transport Museum at Cultra on the Bangor line to which the Museum is connected by a siding.

1955 Happenings (1)

Sutton Coldfield Rail Crash
17 killed and over 20 injured as York-Bristol Express derails on curve approaching Sutton Coldfield station.   *23 January*

1955 Modernisation Plan
BTC publish British Railways Modernisation Plan - includes steam replacement and re-signalling proposals   *24 January*

The USSR ends war with Germany
Presidium of the Supreme Soviet confirms end of war declared in 1941   *25 January*

HMS Ark Royal
Commisioned by the Royal Navy, following completion of fitting out, five years after her launch from Cammel Laird's yards in 1950. She replaced the carrier of the same name torpedoed off Gibralter in 1941 *25 February*

US President Eisenhower
sends first military advisors to South Vietnam   *February*

Pakistan International Airlines
The Government of Pakistan forms National flag carrier   *15 March*

Major Rail Strike starts
UK union A.S.L.E.F. calls members out on strike   *29 March*

PM Resigns
Winston Spencer Churchill resigns as UK Prime Minister replaced the following day by Anthony Eden   *5/6 April*

Fire at Nuclear Plant
Graphite core fire at Windscale, Cumbria   *10 October*

Left: **BELFAST** WT Class 2-6-4T No 7 was a bit of a wanderer. It worked on the Bangor line in 1952/53 in the period of transition towards the full diesel service. It was then used on the GNR system in 1954/55. No 7 is seen here at Great Victoria Street beside one of the GNR's many 4-4-0s. Qs class No 122 was built by the North British Locomotive Company in Glasgow in 1903 and was originally named Vulcan. It was withdrawn by the UTA in 1960.

From Ireland to Island - The Isle of Man

Regulars to the series who have purchased *Railways & Recollections Isle of Man 1964* (No 5 in the series) may be interested in comparing the following views taken nine years earlier.

Above: **DOUGLAS** This view, taken from the signal box on the approach to the station on 15 August 1955, finds No 16 *Mannin* at the water tower between duties. The scene has changed drastically over the ensuing years, as have the services that once graced this jewel in the narrow gauge crown. In 2009 trains still depart from the terminus but sadly the routes from here to Peel, Ramsey and Foxdale via St Johns have long since *departed* from the railway map. However thanks to the IOM government's Department of Transport & Tourism one can still enjoy the pleasures of the steam railway along the scenic route to Port Erin - highly recommended if you are visiting the island.

ST. JOHNS With steam to spare, and being admired by the young enthusiast travelling First Class on the adjacent train, one of the three original locomotives No 1 *Sutherland*, built by Beyer Peacock in 1873, prepares to leave on a train to Peel. This route passed into history in 1968, however No 1 *Sutherland* survives and is displayed at the Port Erin museum.

1955 Happenings (2)

The Vatican
Vatican Radio starts
broadcasting   *26 October*

Battery Railcars for BR announced
by Sir Ian Bolton at Glasgow Press
Conference (Nos 79998/9) for use on the
Aberdeen to Ballater line   *15 October*

The Lovell Telescope
The Lovell Radio Telescope
enters service at Jodrell Bank   *October*

West Germany
West Germany becomes a Federal State,
and four days later joins NATO   *5/9 May*

Warsaw Pact
USSR and communist bloc countries sign
mutual defence treaty   *14 May*

Austria regains sovereignty
The four post WWII occupying forces sign
Austrian State Treaty   *19 May*

State of Emergency in UK
Continuing rail strike prompts declaration
of 'state of emergency'   *31 May*

Tradgedy at Le Mans
Austin Healy and Mercedes collide. Eighty
three killed and over 100 injured *11 June*

Rail strike ends
UK union A.S.L.E.F. agree return to work
strike finaly ends   *14 June*

Last female hanging in UK
Ruth Ellis is hanged at Holloway Prison for
the murder of David Blakely   *13 July*

DOUGLAS The largest locomotive on the railway No 16 *Mannin* is seen resting outside the locoshed at Douglas on 18 August.

Delivered from Beyer Peacock in 1926 this locomotive was considerably more powerful than the previous additions to the fleet.

Ordered out of a need to handle heavier loadings on summer season passenger trains out of Douglas, No 16 proved capable of handling most services without the need for banking or double-heading for the climb up to Port Soderick, the first station on the route to Port Erin.

IOM LOCATION UNKNOWN!
Readers may recognise the location, but your authors have drawn a blank - although we have a number of ideas! Truth be told Ray Ruffell most unusually did not record any details on the original print. However having remarked on the heavier summer loadings in the previous caption we felt this shot captured that event rather well. Here a nine coach train, *at least,* is in evidence and is either being hauled or possibly banked, again this is unclear - was Ray looking forward or back? The answers are no doubt out there so please do let us know...

Below: **BALLAUGH** No 12 *Hutchinson* has now arrived at the picturesque station at Ballaugh and the Guard unloads the goods from the luggage section at the rear of the train. Meanwhile at the front the driver busies himself with oiling and greasing duties - he pauses however to glance across at the camera, giving a cheerful smile. No 12 was outshopped from Beyer, Peacock & Co's Gorton works in Manchester in 1908 and had therefore been in service for some 47 years by the time this photo was captured on 18 August 1955.

Above: **ST. JOHNS** Patience is a virtue! The driver of No 12 *Hutchinson* en route from Douglas to Ramsey awaits the signal from the Guard that all is well to proceed from St. Johns. The Guard's compartment next to the engine is destined to be at the back of the train on the return journey, lest we should think that the Guard should have to run from the back of the train to the front! One imagines that a second Guard's compartment is on hand for him at the back of the train.

Left: **GLEN WYLLIN VIADUCT**
Anyone for bowls? Back in 1955 Glen Wyllin was a mecca for tourists and trippers having been developed by The Manx Northern Railway following the arrival of the railway in 1879. There were pleasure grounds with tennis courts, bowling green, boating lake and of course the beach. Sadly the line closed in 1968 and all that remains of the viaduct are the two towering pillars. The beach remains popular and there is a camp site, toilets and shower block, plus a children's play area.
Crossing the viaduct on the afternoon of 24 August 1955 is a two coach train to Ramsey the loco number was not recorded nor for that matter was the winners name of the bowls match!

Right: **Nr RAMSEY** 'Rattling round the bend' reads the caption on the back of the original print. Tram Car No 1 of the Manx Electric Railway and an unidentified trailer car positively lean into the bend approaching Ramsey - *as if such cambering were a modern invention!* The driver clearly has a wary eye on Ray Ruffell as he approaches.

Like no less than twenty two other cars supplied to the company between 1888 and 1902, Tram Car No 1, built in 1893, was a product of George F. Milnes & Co Ltd from Birkenhead and latterly of Hadley, Shropshire. The company supplied many other concerns including Manchester, Blackburn, Bournemouth & Poole and one may even have reached Chile!* The 34 seater tram rides on trucks built by Brush Electrical Engineering Ltd at their Lambeth (closed c1914) or Loughborough plant. The tram's electric motors were made by Societe l'Electricite et l'Hydraulique, Charleroi, Belgium - one might therefore conclude that Tram Car No 1 is a truly international vehicle!
(Company Catalogue illustration 1900)*

RAMSEY Here we see a more detailed view of Tram Car No 1 having arrived at Ramsey station. The driver's overcoat hangs on the hook above his wooden stool and just inside the car can be seen that seating was of the wooden slats variety - no cushioned comfort here then. The overall appearance of this picture gives your authors the impression of Rio de Janeiro rather than Ramsey, with palm trees and the fine, upstanding, coffee plantation owneresque, gentleman surveying the scene before him...

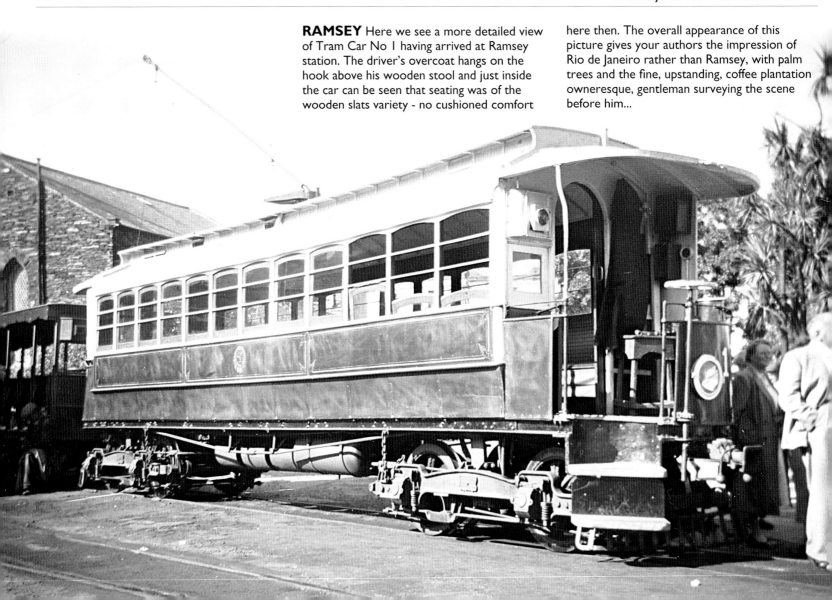

Cambrian Coast Wanderings

BARMOUTH The Barmouth Bridge is a single-track, largely wooden railway viaduct crossing the estuary of the Afon Mawddach in Gwynedd. Pedestrians can walk the 900 yards on a footbridge incorporated on the landward side alongside the track across the river on payment of a toll. Built by the Aberystwyth and Welsh Coast Railway, it opened in 1867 and, as built, included a lifting drawbridge section to permit the passage of tall ships. Situated at the northern end of the bridge, this was rebuilt in 1901 as a swing bridge with two steel spans; this facility is still available but

rarely used. On 22 July, No 2286 prepares to cross the bridge on its way south towards Machynlleth.

Passenger train services over the bridge declined significantly during the 1960s, when local connecting lines were closed, causing all traffic to take a longer route from Shrewsbury, via Machynlleth. Due to an attack

by the toredo marine worm, serious doubts arose in 1980 concerning safety under the weight of modern locomotives and this led to a ban on locomotive-hauled trains, causing the immediate cessation of the diminishing freight traffic north of Tywyn, including explosives traffic to and from the factory at Penrhyndeudraeth. *Gerald Adams, MJS collection*

1955 Happenings (3)

Stirling Moss
At last the British Grand Prix is won by a British Driver as Stirling takes the chequred flag to win at Aintree Circuit   23 July

The Ffestiniog Railway
reopens but as the UK's first
Preserved Railway   23 July

High in the sky
English Electric Canberra sets new World altitude record - 65,876 ft   29 August

The Guiness Book of Records
published for the first time   27 August

Vladimir Nabokov
The famous novel *Lolita* is first published in Paris   15 September

Newsreaders seen on UK TV!
Richard Baker, Keneth Kendall and Robert Dougall appear on screen for the first time reading the BBC News   September

UK Commercial TV begins
ITV broadcasts begin   22 September

Princess Margaret
announces that she will not marry Group Captain Peter Townsend   October

Fire at Nuclear Plant
Graphite core fire at
Windscale, Cumbria   10 October

Battery Railcars for BR announced
by Sir Ian Bolton at Glasgow
Press Conference (Nos 79998/9)
for use on the Aberdeen to
Ballater line   15 October

PWLLHELI Pictured at this north west Wales terminus on 21 July, the fireman and driver, who is conscious of the photographer, seem to be enjoying some joke, as the locomotive is prepared before returning along the Cambrian Coast line to Machynlleth. Commonly referred to as 'Dukedogs', from their mongrel creation with parts of '*Duke of Cornwall*' and '*Bulldog*' classes, No 9024 was thus 'born' on 1 February 1939, with the frames of No 3409 and was numbered 3224 until receiving what would become its BR number on 7 September 1946. Shedded at Shrewsbury when the railways were nationalised in 1948, a move to Machynlleth was soon decreed and there it stayed until withdrawal on 30 September 1957, spending its life handling the local passenger workings along the ex-Cambrian lines.
Gerald Adams, MJS collection

PWLLHELI Another 'Dukedog', this time seen on 2 August, waiting for the 'off' and the the very pleasant but, in places, precarious run along the Cambrian Coast. No 9020 was manufactured on 21 November 1938 on frames from No 3414 and was originally No 3220. The number that it took into BR days was bestowed on 1 August 1946. Oswestry was its shed for many years before moving to Bristol (Bath Road) on 24 January 1953. Its stay there was not overly long, however and it trundled back to the Principality on 17 July 1954, to Machynlleth. Its stay there was just four days short of exactly three years, whence it became another ex-loco! Note that here, over a year from its return from Bristol, it is still wearing the now incorrectly applied 82A shedplate! *Gerald Adams, MJS collection*

Left: **PORTHMADOG** As will be seen on p.25, the first design by Churchward for his '4500 Class' was for a straight-topped tank. In 1927, he introduced a refinement of the tank shape, to give a higher profile, for greater capacity, and incorporating a sloping front to the tank top. It also increased its weight by 4 tons, to 61 tons. This deviation became known as the '4575 Class' and the first of this design is captured on film here on a dull 21 July, at Porthmadog, on its way to Pwllheli and bearing the lamp code for 'ordinary' or local passenger train. Another long-standing servant of the area, No 4575 spent much of its time working from Machynlleth shed, until February 1960, when it moved to Bristol (Bath Road). However, the stay was short and just four months later it was back again, but just for two months, with its demise coming on 13 August of that year. *Gerald Adams, MJS collection*

Right: **PWLLHELI** As well as actually hauling trains, a not inconsiderable amount of shunting was also required in steam days, especially with the freight duties. On 25 July, No 4555 fiddles around Pwllheli yard in the hot summer sunshine with a solitary box van. Initially introduced from 1906, Churchward's design was for branch line and general cross country work it was a development of his '4400 Class' 2-6-2Ts, with 6" larger wheels. Built in 1924, No 4555 has the original straight-topped tanks and was a regular on the Cambrian routes until October 1957, when it

PWLLHELI

transferred into England, to Westbury. Devon and Cornwall became its home from 1959, with stays at Newton Abbot, St Blazey and Plymouth (Laira) sheds. It was withdrawn from the latter on 30 November 1963 and happily escaped the grim reaper, being sold for preservation on the Paignton & Dartmouth Steam Railway. *Gerald Adams, MJS collection*

Locos On Shed

Left: **PWLLHELI** Steam loco sheds were many and various in shape, size, design and condition and the latter looks to be giving some cause for concern in this view of No 9008 on 25 July! The second of three sheds to serve the area, this facility opened in 1907, replacing the ex-1867 timber building that was demolished to allow for an extension of the line into the town. By this date in 1955, this 'later' version, built of corrugated iron with a slated gable-style pitched roof, was very dilapidated and it was subsequently demolished. Its replacement, doubling the number of roads, of brick construction was opened in 1958, but only to survive until 1966! No 9008 was 'new' on 10 February 1937, built on frames from No 3403, numbered 3208 prior to 1946 and was named *Earl Bathurst*. Withdrawal was from Machynlleth on 13 July 1957.
Gerald Adams, MJS collection

Opposite top: **PWLLHELI** Another straight-topped tank (see p.25) is seen on shed at Pwllheli on 25 July. No 4549 is between duties and runs towards the turntable, to be watered from the tower on the far side and then to be turned so as to be facing the correct way for the return journey along the Cambrian Coast. Like many of its sisters, No 4549 was another to have served for many years in this part of Wales before departing to Devon and Cornwall. The move away to England came in February 1960 in this case, with transfer to Laira shed in Plymouth. Its stay there and at subsequent homes was short – four months at Laira, three at Penzance, nine at Truro and a final six back at Penzance. Many branches saw visits but its end came comparatively early, on 30 December 1961. *Gerald Adams, MJS collection*

Below: **PORTHMADOG** The date is 21 July and the photographer has been graced with co-operation by the shed foreman – pictured – who has allowed the 'Standard Class 2' No 78000 to moved out from the shed interior to be captured on film. It here stands proudly at the head of a short row for its portrait, in the company of three ex-GWR 'Class 4575' 2-6-2Ts. New in November 1952 - to Oswestry - it is here allocated to Machynlleth shed and was, thus, a common sight along the Cambrian Coast metals. Moving to Nottingham in May 1963 – and Derby eight months later – it was withdrawn from the latter on 17 July 1965, less than thirteen years old! The final step to becoming a candidate for transformation to baked bean tins was from Cashmore's, Great Bridge, Birmingham, scrapyard in December of that year.
Gerald Adams, MJS collection

1955 No 1 Records

January

The Finger of Suspicion	*Dickie Valentine*
Mambo Italiano	*Rosemary Clooney*
The Finger of Suspicion (*again*)	*Dickie Valentine*

February

The Finger of Suspicion	*Dickie Valentine*
Mambo Italiano (*again*)	*Rosemary Clooney*
Softly, Softly	*Ruby Murray*

March

| Softly, Softly | *Ruby Murray* |
| Give me your word | *Tennessee Ernie Ford* |

April

| Give me your word | *Tennessee Ernie Ford* |
| Cherry pink and apple blossom white | *Perez Prado* |

May

Cherry pink and apple blossom white	*Perez Prado*
Stranger in paradise	*Tony Bennett*
Cherry pink and apple blossom white	*Eddie Calvert*

June

| Cherry pink and apple blossom white | *Eddie Calvert* |
| Unchained melody | *Jimmy Young* |

July

Unchained melody	*Jimmy Young*
Dreamboat	*Alma Cogan*
Rose Marie	*Slim Whitman*

August

| Rose Marie | *Slim Whitman* |

September

| Rose Marie | *Slim Whitman* |

October

| Rose Marie | *Slim Whitman* |
| The Man from Laramie | *Jimmy Young* |

November

The Man from Laramie	*Jimmy Young*
Hernando's hideaway	*Johnston Brothers*
Rock around the clock	*Bill Hailey and His Comets*

December

| Rock around the clock | *Bill Hailey and His Comets* |
| Christmas Alphabet | *Dickie Valentine* |

WIDNEY MANOR The station was opened by the GWR in 1899, to serve the eponymous area of Solihull. Into the 21st century, it is managed by London Midland under that company's franchise and is also served by Chiltern Rail trains and has been subject to much variety over the years, in motive power and stock both serving it and passing through. Being on the erstwhile Birkenhead-Paddington, via Wolverhampton (Low Level), through route, it saw predominantly ex-GW-type of locomotives, even into BR days. Thus, the sight of one of Stanier's massive 'Coronations', built for the LMS, through the station would have been distinctly unusual. Perhaps, therefore, this view of No 46237 *City of Bristol*, on 30 April, on what is obviously a prestigious working, with carriage name boards in place, heading for Birmingham, is likely to owe more to the need for a diversion from its normal route than a routine visit. Note the relatively modern, semi-detached housing in the distance; the goods shed beyond the second coach; and the tall, repeater signal, indicating the imminent arrival of a train on the nearest tracks.
Gerald Adams, MJS collection

WIDNEY MANOR was the next station south of Solihull, on the outskirts of Birmingham, on the ex-GWR route to Leamington Spa. More often heavy with local and/or commuter traffic, it also saw its fair share of express workings. On 30 April, No 4076 *Carmarthen Castle* storms into the station with a Weymouth-Birmingham (Snow Hill) service, watched by just two waiting

Birmingham Beckons...

passengers on the platform. One of the 1923 Collett design, developed from the earlier 'Star Class' 4-6-0s, No 4076 was an Old Oak Common resident when inherited by British Railways in 1948, but would subsequently wander widely – to Chester, Newton Abbot – its home when seen here – Landore (on the outskirts of Swansea) and, finally, Llanelli. The end came on 9 February 1963.
Gerald Adams, MJS collection

WIDNEY MANOR Moments later from the previous page and we have consist of a very different kind. Partly hidden from view by the smoke from the locomotive, an un-fitted freight disturbs the peace on 30 April behind No 6864 *Dymock Grange*. A well travelled engine, No 6864 spent the first seven years of BR life at Reading shed, before moving to Oxford for the next four years. Thereafter, sojourns were at Penzance, Bristol (St Philip's Marsh), Banbury and Tyseley, from where condemnation came on 9 October 1965. Cutting was swiftly undertaken, at G Cohen's, Kingsbury site two months later.
Gerald Adams, MJS collection

Below: **WIDNEY MANOR** Immediately to the north of the station, the line crosses a local road, supported by a strong steel bridge. This can be seen on either side of the tracks as we view No 6959 *Peatling Hall*, heading south from the Birmingham area with a decidedly mixed freight. Collett's 'Halls' had been introduced in numbers from 1928 and had given valiant service thereafter. During WWII, however, it was decided that there was a need for more and Hawksworth modified the design with larger superheater and design changes to frames and bogies. *Peatling Hall* was the first to appear, with this new 'sub-class' known as 'Modified Halls'. Working from the London area sheds for most of its life, it was serving Old Oak Common at this date and was withdrawn on 15 Janaury 1966, a result of the end of steam on the ex-GWR routes. It was scrapped two months later, at Cashmore's Newport yard. *Gerald Adams, MJS collection*

Bordesley - same signals different motive power...

Below: **BORDESLEY** Running south from the centre of Birmingham, Bordesley was the first station after Birmingham Moor Street and was the site of a large marshalling yard , the north end of which was crossed by an ex-LMS line. On 13 August, No 5339 is pressed into service to head yet another summer Saturday holiday 'extra' and is seen approaching the station area. No doubt the driver, as he leans from the cab in this view, will be somewhat

relieved to be soon stopping at Birmingham (Snow Hill) station, in the centre of the Metropolis. With the loco's allocation being Newton Abbot at this time, it is probable that the train is from the West Country. *Gerald Adams, MJS collection*

Below left: **BORDESLEY** As well as having to contend with all the extras on a summer Saturday, the signalman had also to look after freight workings and then, in addition, to fit in light engine loco movements. One such is here portrayed, as No 5166 and No 3693 run between duties, no doubt linked together to prevent unnecessary blocking of the lines. No 5166 was a long-term Tyseley engine and stayed there until moving south in November 1957, to Severn Tunnel Junction, from where the end came on 20 May 1961. Also a Tyseley loco at this date - and another long-term servant of this shed - No 3693 moved into deepest southwest Wales in May 1960. Its demise was on 20 July 1964, from Gloucester (Horton Road) shed, to where it had transferred for its last 12 months of life.
Gerald Adams, MJS collection

Below right: **BORDESLEY.** Summer Saturday traffic was often heavy, not least the holiday trains and it was frequently hard work for the operating staff, to provide locomotives, carriages, train paths, etc. On the ex-GWR routes, services to and from Devon and Cornwall were greatly expanded on these days and such is a view here, on 13 August. Twin 'Moguls' No 5341 and No 5322 have their work cut out as they work an 'extra' past

Bordesley station, a task they would have taken on northwards from Stratford-on-Avon station. No 5341 was the younger of the two, but was the first to go, on 11 July 1959. The more ancient No 5322 came to its shed to replace it, previously having been in the London area, including just over two months at Didcot, and lasted until 4 May 1964. Having been saved for preservation, it is appropriate that it has returned to its 'home' at Didcot, where it has given pleasure to very many visitors.
Gerald Adams, MJS collection

Right: **TYSELEY** It was not just in the latter days of steam that the locomotives looked distinctly work weary and down at heel. Even in these days of relative normality for BR steam in 1955, the grime was just as prevalent. A filthy No 2872 draws to a halt, against adverse signals (out of sight to the left) on 6 August, alongside the station, with a rake of mixed vintage coal wagons. Note the grounded coach for staff accommodation to the left; the triple signal gantry; tall telegraph pole; and the buildings of the engine shed beyond. When oil burning in early 1948, No 2872 was numbered 4800, but reverted to its original number in November of that year. Serving for much of its life in South Wales, it saw the end in August 1963. *Gerald Adams, MJS collection*

Right: **TYSELEY** A bright sunny day sees ex-GWR 'Grange' No 6804 *Brockington Grange* steaming through the station with a holiday special, on 6 August. The station looks at peace as the express passes, with the neat and tidy appearance, coupled with paintwork in good order, and a tank engine shunting lazily to the left. The loco bears the reporting code in true GWR style, making it absolutely clear to signalmen which service is in hand. *Gerald Adams, MJS collection*

BIRMINGHAM (Snow Hill) When first opened by the GWR in 1852, the station was known as Livery Street, but was renamed six years later. Initially a simple affair, it was rebuilt in 1871, to cope with longer trains, with a huge arched roof of iron and glass and a simple wooden overhead bridge linking the two platforms. More substantial was the redevelopment of 1906 (completed in 1912), which set out to challenge the domination of nearby New Street station of the L&NWR. This served the locality well for the next fifty years, until the 'Beeching Axe' laid waste to the services and then the station, which closed in 1972 and was demolished in 1977. Happily, the site was reopened a decade later, but in much reduced format, 'buried' under a multi-storey car park. In happier times, on 6 August, No 4998 *Eyton Hall* drifts into the station with yet another summer Saturday service, but the young lad, left, seems to be more interested in the photographer! *Gerald Adams, MJS collection*

BIRMINGHAM (Snow Hill) The date is 21 May and at around 1.30 p.m., No 2516 bursts into the light from the gloom of Snow Hill station, with a SLS (Midland Area) afternoon trip to Cleobury Mortimer. Whilst still on BR's books, time was running out for this loco, with the end coming less than year later, on 21 April 1956. Another veteran of ex-Cambrian routes, with long stays at Oswestry shed, it became popular for railtours in its latter days. For this tour, it had its front number and shedplate painted out in black and the number painted on the bufferbeam, to represent its erstwhile GWR status. Appearing from Swindon Works in March 1897, it escaped the cutter's torch, to be officially preserved and entombed in the Great Western Railway Museum in Swindon.
Gerald Adams, MJS collection

1955 Happenings (4)

Austria
Following the withdrawal of the last allied troops following WWII Austria declares permanent neutrality status   *26 October*

The Lovell Telescope
The Lovell Radio Telescope enters service at Jodrell Bank   *October*

Vietnam
Declares itself a Republic   *26 October*

The Vatican
Vatican Radio starts broadcasting   *26 October*

Below: **BIRMINGHAM (Snow Hill)**
The following day and the loco (originally
numbered 4814) is still in much the same
position, but this time seen from the opposite
side of the track to that above. Sadly, this was
not one of the lucky members of the class to
be preserved, but four have survived and can
often be seen on heritage lines recreating the
push-pull services of their past.
Gerald Adams, MJS collection

Above: **BIRMINGHAM (Snow Hill)**
One of the delights of standing on a station
in steam days, especially a large one or a
terminus, was to see the shunting of stock and/
or the appearance of more diminutive locos.
Both are portrayed here, as No 1414 busies
itself around the station with an auto coach on
21 March. Built by Collett in the early 1930s,
they were fitted with push-pull apparatus, to
enable them to work shuttle trains over short
distances or on lightly laid branch lines. No
1414 was stationed at Stourbridge Junction shed
for the whole of its BR lifespan and enjoyed
much time on the short trip to and from
Junction to Town stations. Withdrawal came
on 20 April 1957. *Gerald Adams, MJS collection*

Out and about in The Midlands, Scotland and The North

Left: **LEAMINGTON SPA** On your marks....! It would seem that No 6118 *(left)* and No 6949 *Haberfield Hall* are under starters orders as they stand shoulder to shoulder ahead of their respective passenger rakes on 23 April, but the lamp codes give the game away. No 6118 bears the indication of light engine, so is perhaps backing up to the coaching stock, ready to couple and the code will then be changed. By contrast, the 'Hall' is coupled and displays the code for empty coaching stock, so perhaps it has hauled a service that has terminated here and has had the code changed ready for a move to the carriage sidings. *Gerald Adams, MJS collection*

1955 Arrivals & Departures

Births

Rowan Atkinson	*comedian*	6 January
Kevin Costner	*actor*	18 January
Simon Rattle	*conductor*	19 January
Nicolas Sarkozy	*French President*	28 January
Kirsty Wark	*TV presenter*	9 February
Greg Norman	*golfer*	10 February
Steve Jobs	*c.e.o.Apple Computers Inc*	24 February
Bruce Willis	*actor*	19 March
Janice Long	*radio disc jockey*	5 April
Olga Korbut	*gymnast*	16 May
Paul O'Grady	*comedian/TV presenter*	14 June
Allan Border	*cricketer*	27 July
Janet Ellis	*TV presenter*	16 September
Timmy Mallett	*TV presenter*	18 October

Deaths

Sir Alexander Fleming	*scientist*	(b. 1881)	11 March
Charlie Parker	*saxophonist*	(b. 1920)	12 March
Albert Einstein	*physicist*	(b. 1879)	18 April
James Dean	*actor*	(b. 1931)	30 September
Alfred Carpenter VC	*RN Officer*	(b. 1881)	27 December

Opposite page: **BANBURY** For slightly heavier shuttle work than could be accommodated by the '1400 Class', Collett introduced the '5400s', again push-pull fitted, but with six coupled wheels instead of four and a tractive effort of 14700 lbs, as opposed to 13900. On 23 April, No 5409 stands in the main down platform at Banbury, with the driver sharing a joke with a colleague before his next job. Interestingly, the loco here bears an 84C shedplate – denoting allocation to the local shed – but official records indicate it to have been transferred from Southall to Neasden, on the Eastern Region, on 22 May 1954! There is no record of a transfer to Banbury and, perhaps, it was merely an unrecorded loan. It was withdrawn from Neasden on 13 June 1959. It had previously received a black lined livery at Wolverhampton Works on 14 August 1949. *Gerald Adams, MJS collection*

Right: **BANBURY** At its height and up to 1966, Banbury was a mini-hub of lines, with trains arriving from the south from Marylebone (via Bicester), Paddington (via Oxford) and Cheltenham (via Kingham) and from the north from Birmingham and from the northeast, by way of a branch connection to the ex-GCR close to Woodford Halse. The latter is advertised on the station board, with the rather enigmatic message 'Change here for the Eastern Region'!

On 23 April, No 6906 *Chicheley Hall* coasts gently into the down platform, with an

unidentified northbound fitted freight – possibly bound for that Eastern Region branch. Note that the running-in board has had the suffix 'General' painted beneath the raised letters of the town's name. The station was more or less as built at this date, but would undergo a massive modernisation within the next four years. *Gerald Adams, MJS collection*

Top left: **BANBURY** Showing another link with the Eastern Region, No 60871 hurries light engine through the station, with a clear road to run beyond the road bridge and clear the main line. It has probably arrived with an inter-regional train from the northeast and will have given over its train to a Western Region loco. It was not common to see a 'V2' at Banbury, so this would have been a real 'cop' for local spotters. *Gerald Adams, MJS collection*

Bottom left: **LEICESTER (Central)** Moments before all the excitement of the arrival of 'The Master Cutler', the station rested quietly, with 'B1' No 61181 also waiting, on the western side of the large station, for its turn to work, perhaps to shunt the coaching stock behind it. Progressive emasculation of the GCR route occurred after takeover by Midland Region in the late 1950s, to the extent that the whole route closed to through traffic just eleven years from this view. *Gerald Adams, MJS collection*

Leicester Central 2 - 1 Leicester Midland

Bottom left: **LEICESTER (Central)** Having metaphorically travelled up the GCR route from Banbury, our photographer has arrived at another loco changeover point. On 21 June, the northbound 'The Master Cutler', Marylebone-Sheffield (Victoria) is changing 'horses'. 'B1' No 61136 has just arrived from the 'smoke' and prepares to leave its coaches, after the 100-mile run and hand over to No

60855 – another 'V2'. A prestigious train for the route at the time, it would be switched away, to run on the ECML before the decade was out. *Gerald Adams, MJS collection*

Below: **LEICESTER (Midland)** For one of your authors, this picture is very poignant, for he spent many hours on or around Leicester's London Road station and oft times watched this locomotive bustling around the area, shunting coaching stock and wagons, or merely

waiting to be of assistance wherever needed. No 41268 was new on 9 September 1950 and went straight to Leicester, where it stayed until 14 February 1959. It then moved to its only other home – Liverpool's Bank Hall shed – until dispensed with on 11 July 1964, a victim of changing fashions and ideas on our railways. Seen here on 23 June, it is taking a break between shunting duties, for its tanks to be refreshed. Into the 21st century, all the sidings to the right have gone, to make way for the ubiquitous car park (!), and the view to the left has also changed, both on and off the railway. *Gerald Adams, MJS collection*

Below: **HEANOR** A century ago, Heanor, in Derbyshire, boasted two stations – one built by the Midland Railway, sometimes known as Heanor North, on a branch from Ripley to Shipley Gate, and Heanor Gate, terminus of a branch from Ilkeston on the Great Northern Railway's Derbyshire Extension line. Of the two, the latter had the more major facilities and lasted the longest. The Midland station closed to passengers in 1926 and to freight on 1 September 1951; whereas the GNR terminus served passengers until 1939 and goods handling until 7 October 1963. A visit during 1955 shows this terminus in declining state, devoid of station nameboard, weeds proliferating on the platform surface, but obviously still busy with freight duties. Note the imposing double doors at the end of the station building. *J H Turner, MJS collection*

Right: **EDINBURGH (St Margaret's)** Edinburgh was served by two major sheds, to handle the needs of Waverley station, Haymarket to the west and St Margaret's to the east. The first facility at the latter, a stone built circular roundhouse, was opened in 1846 and lasted almost to its centenary, but was demolished after a fire in 1944. A second shed, this time a straight, dead end shed, was constructed on the opposite side of the main line in 1866 and this was further augmented by a square roundhouse in 1871. This last was also demolished during the last War – in 1942 – to make way for more siding space and turntable. The remaining remnants of the three were closed

on 1 May 1967. In slightly happier times, No 56035 stands outside the shed in May 1955, complete with its ancient wooden attachment, acting as coal carrying tender for the hungry boiler! Newly arrived here, it had previously served across Scotland, at Greenock. It went back there in July 1957 and was finally withdrawn on 28 August 1960. *Gerald Adams, MJS collection*

Opposite inset left: **HUNTINGDON** South of the station, No 60026 *Miles Beevor* accelerates past a ganger with its top link express, bound for London. The ex-MR line to Kettering can be seen on the lower level to the right. *Eric Sawford, MJS collection*

Inset far right: **LEEDS CITY.** Whilst an all-over trainshed is desirable to protect waiting travellers from the elements, it was not conducive to a rapid dispersion of smoke and steam. No 61448 illustrates the point on 11 November, as it draws to a halt with a service from York. *MJS collection*

STAVELEY (Central) was part of the Great Central Railway's route from Nottingham (Victoria) to Sheffield (Victoria) and was situated slightly to the northeast of Chesterfield. On a murky day, an unidentified ex-LNER 'B1' leaves the station, with typical LNER coaching stock in tow immediately behind the tender. *MJS collection*

FRASERBURGH Back into Scotland, we are on the north coast of Aberdeenshire. The station was the terminus of a GNoSR line from Maud Junction and formed a junction with a small coastal branch line from St Combs (which opened in 1903). Fraserburgh railway station opened in 1865 and closed to passengers late in 1965 – six months after local stations and the branches to St Combs and Peterhead – and the site has been redeveloped. Freight continued at the site until 1979, after which the track was lifted. However, the GNoSR engine shed and BR goods offices remain in alternative

uses. On 29 March 1955, No 46460 and No 61294 stand outside that shed, alongside a rake of empty coal wagons. No 46460 was new in June 1950 and started work at St Margaret's shed, in Edinburgh. Subsequent work was in the Aberdeenshire and Perth shed areas, before a final to move southwest, to Ayr, on 30 October 1965, from where the end came eleven months later. It was scrapped at Motherwell Machinery & Scrap Co, Wishaw in December 1966. Note the impressive church overseeing it all! *B K B Green, MJS collection*

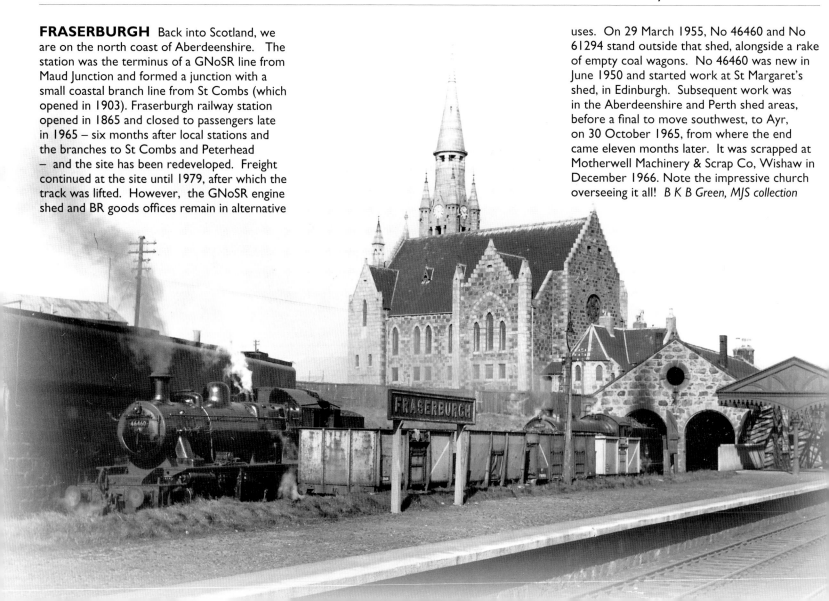

BASSENTHWAITE LAKE Roughly mid-way along the line that bisected Cumbria, from Penrith to Workington, the station stood alongside the lake at its northern end. The route was originally the creation of the Cockermouth, Keswick & Penrith Railway and made connection with the LNWR at both ends. The line opened to goods traffic on October 26th, 1864 , and to passengers on January 5th, 1865, but the CK&PR was never the operating railway. The route suffered like so many others post-War and was threatened with complete closure. However, in an attempt to stave off the evil day Derby Lightweight diesel multiple-units were introduced on January 3rd, 1955 to work the passenger services, this immediately leading to increases in profits. Just six months later one such unit arrives at the delightful station and the beauty and sheer majesty of the surrounding area is readily apparent.
MJS collection

1955
Happenings (3)

Laika in space
Russians launch Sputnik II carrying Laika the first dog in space   *3 November*

New Zealand
The Rimutaka Tunnel opens, at over 5 miles in length it was the longest in the country on opening.   *3 November*

Plane Crash on Isle of Wight
Solent flying boat on route from Southampton to Lisbon and Madeira crashes at Chessel Down   *15 November*

Rail Crash
Milton Nr Didcot in Oxfordshire - Britannia Class No 70026 *Polar Star* and train derail on crossover   *20 November*

Rail Crash
Waterloo to Windsor electric unit collides with freight train at Barnes   *2 December*

Lewisham Rail Crash
Cannon Street to Ramsgate Express colides with Charing Cross to Hayes EMU - 92 killed   *4 December*

First US Satellite fails to lift off
rocket explodes on launch pad   *6 December*

Clement Atlee resigns
as leader of the Labour party. Hugh Gaitskell takes over   *7/14 December*

Heathrow Airport
The Queen's Building inaugurated by Her Majesty The Queen   *16 December*

HOLMFIRTH Home of Nora Batty, 'Compo', Norman Clegg, et al, they sadly would never have had the chance to sample a train journey! The branch line to Holmfirth was built at the same time as the Huddersfield and Sheffield Junction Railway line from Huddersfield to Penistone, with engineering works to the same double line standard, in anticipation of a widespread industrialisation that never materialised. The line ran for 1¾ miles, leaving the main line south of Brockholes and curving south through Thongsbridge – the only intermediate station – before ending in a single platform terminus (with a turntable) at Holmfirth. The goods shed and sidings can be seen to the right of this view from August 1955. The traffic was obviously not heavy at this time, as the staff have time to spare, to accommodate the photographer's wishes and to have their portrait taken – the branch closed on 3 May 1965. A little over 5½ years old when seen here, No 41250 had first been resident at Wakefield shed, but, as can be seen from the 25F shedplate, was now a member of Low Moor's stud. Withdrawn from Copley Hill on 7 December 1963, it was not a particularly good investment for the railway, at just 14 years and four days old! *MJS collection*

Index